BIG PROPS

Osprey Colour Series

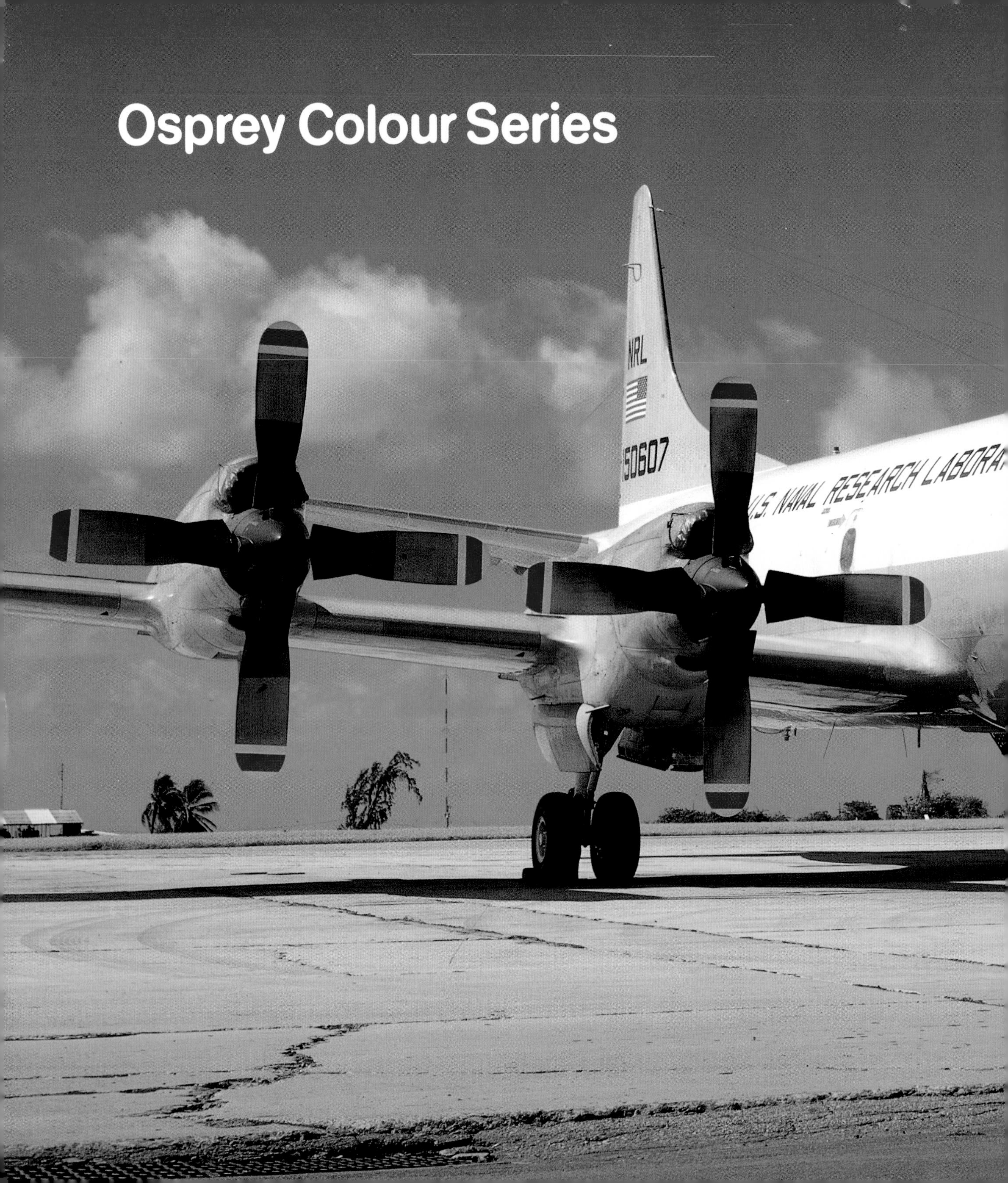

BIG PROPS

Austin J Brown
and Mark R Wagner

Published in 1987 by Osprey Publishing Limited
27A Floral Street, London WC2E 9DP
Member company of the George Philip Group

British Library Cataloguing in Publication Data

Big props.—(Osprey colour series).
    1. Transport planes—History
    I. Brown, Austin J.   II. Wagner, Mark R.
    629.133′343   TL685.4
ISBN 0-85045-801-3

Editor Dennis Baldry
Designed by Norman Brownsword
Printed in Hong Kong

Front cover 28-year-old Virgin Viscount G-BAPG on approach to Gatwick's Runway 08 in March 1986 whilst on lease from British Air Ferries to operate the Maastrict connection with Richard Branson's new transatlantic service

Title pages Distinctive paddle blades absorb the 4500 ehp from each of the Allison T56 turboprops on this US Naval Research Lab P-3 Orion parked at Grantly Adams International, Barbados, in March 1985

Back cover Fairchild C-82A Jet Packet N8009E marooned in a corner of the airfield at Fort Lauderdale, Florida, in 1977. The J34 turbojet mounted above the fuselage provided a welcome shove to help the hard-worked Pratt & Whitney R-2800 engines haul the lumbering Packet off the ground. Packet production ended in 1948 and the aircraft was superseded by the far more capable C-119 Boxcar from December 1949

Hardly built for speed! Air Atlantique's Bristol Freighter clatters to the holding point at—you guessed it—Bristol in October 1984. The old girl is still going strong, unlike the almost equally aged Varsity and Dove in the background

Austin Brown and Mark Wagner run the Aviation Picture Library from their Bristol-based studio in England, and they provide aviation and aerial photographs for advertising, publishing and PR requirements.

The son of a professional photographer, Austin Brown has managed to combine his love of flying with the trade he was brought up in. Trained as a commercial pilot in 1967 by Cambrian Airways, he left the company 10 years later to fly DC-3s in the Caribbean for Air BVI. He still flies as a freelance captain in the UK and West Africa.

Aged 22, Mark Wagner is another photographer/pilot, completing his UK PPL in Portugal with a British instructor during three weeks' vacation in 1984. As a freelance photojournalist he contributes to many international aviation magazines in addition to providing PR and advertising photography for Malaysian Airlines and Asian Aerospace.

The late Stephen Piercey's enthusiasm for the 'Big Props' influenced both photographers, and they have produced this follow-up to *SKY TRUCK* 1 and 2 in their own individual, yet complimentary, styles.

The photographs in *BIG PROPS* were taken with Hasselblad and Nikon cameras, loaded with Fuji and Kodachrome film.

An airport truck belches diesel fumes into the midnight sky as mail is unloaded from a pair of Euroair Heralds at Liverpool in November 1986

Contents

The wings of the dragon

Left The severe terminal building at Lanzhou Zhongchuan Airport, some 6300 ft above sea level—the airport plays host to a resident Il-14, 40 MiG-19 fighters and CAAC's first batch of BAe 146s. **Right** One of the many interesting signs at Xian Airport's main terminal, where spitoons are placed in strategic positions on the floor.
Below The Xian Friendship Store offers a limited range of souvenirs, drinks and nick-nacks to tourists and Communist Party members

Clockwise from extreme top left A composite tour of Lanzhou Zhongchuan: **1** Sign language **2** The flight information blackboard lists aircraft registrations as well as flight numbers **3** Airport fire crew oversee the startup of a Tu-154M from their well kept fire truck **4** Standby passengers: even the Shanghai region, with updated facilities, more aircraft and extra flights, claims that for every 2000 passengers who get a seat about 1000 have to be turned away **5** The baggage lorry weaves a route past various bikes, trikes and aircraft

A typical Chinese ramp scene: aircraft old and new, bicycles, classic trucks, and someone dozing off

Right A 'People' class 4-6-2, the world's final design of steam express passenger locomotive, a type which is still in full production near Shanghai. Steam locomotives are used extensively due to their relatively low operating costs (coal is plentiful in China) compared to diesel traction. Travellers who have experienced train journeys in China speak of soot entering the carriages through open windows, no interior lighting at night, no heating and impassable corridors blocked by passengers without seats. The latter problem is not without parallel on some mainline routes operated by British Rail

Active runways in China seem to have a magnetic attraction for people riding bicycles, and Lanzhou Zhongchuan Airport proved no exception. Occasionally, cyclists waited at the edge of the runway for an aircraft to pass (Il-14, No 607)

Due to its paratrooper-style seating arrangement, Il-14 No 607 offered a generous amount of legroom. The charming stewardess served piping hot jasmine tea and presented the 10 passengers with CAAC sweets and keyrings. Blankets were distributed on boarding and the rather chilly cabin warmed to a more comfortable 12°C an hour after takeoff. The anecdotes about spilt coffee freezing to the carpet in winter must be true!

Above and left Once the passengers had disembarked, No 607 was refuelled and scrutinized for any obvious faults. The aircraft had finished its day's work by lunchtime and moved to a quieter part of the airfield

Left The two 1900 hp Shvetsov ASh-82T 14-cylinder radials slowly oozed oil as No 607 maintained a respectable 260 km/h at 3000 m above sea level, just above the ridges of the Ordos mountains, enroute from Lanzhou to TaiYuan

Below Because the scheduled An-24 flight was overbooked, the Il-14 had to be specially chartered at a cost of nearly 10,000 Yuan (£2000). Having completed the 2 hour 40 minute flight from Lanzhou to TaiYuan, No 607 is prepared for an empty return flight as the passengers retire to the airport restaurant for an octopus lunch

This page Il-14 No 668 on the ramp at Wu Su Airport, TaiYuan, before departing for Xian with ten British, three French and thirteen Chinese passengers. As soon as the trusty Shvetsov's had barked into life the aircraft quickly taxied to the runway for an immediate take off, the benefit of power checks having evidently been dispensed with. During the flight the stewardess handed out small bags of local chocolate, cartons of milk with straws and a wad of booklets in English and Chinese with such titles as *The resolution of the central committee of the Chinese Communist Party on the guiding principles for building a socialist society with an advanced culture and ideology*

Il-14 No 5513 of the Air Force of the People's Liberation Army was one of three AFPLA examples parked at Wu Su Airport in October 1986

Another AFPLA Il-14 (No 5425) with an armed
Red Guard in attendance

Overleaf Displaying the old-style bare metal
CAAC livery, Il-14 No 604 was apparently
awaiting overhaul by the 103rd Aircraft Factory at
Chengdu Airport

Wu Su Airport at TaiYuan was alive with no less than nine Il-14s—three AFPLA and six CAAC. Here (right to left) Nos 668, 648 and Air Force 5513 are parked in a row

Overleaf The no-nonsense wing design of the Il-14 is accentuated in this view of No 648 at Wu Su. **Inset** Unfortunately all requests to visit the flight deck of an active Il-14 were turned down, but No 666 in the Aeronautical Compound at Peking University is open to the public

The old and the new. Parked in a remote corner of Zhongchuan Airport, Il-14 No 604 watches a newly imported Tu-154M, registered B-2604, rotate at the start of a scheduled flight to Peking

Surrounded by trees on the outskirts of Peking at the N an Yuan AFPLA base, this An-12/Yun-8 shared the parking area with four Il-18s, a Trident, a MiG-15, an An-24 and a Canadair Challenger

Above A Chinese woman rides her bicycle down the taxiway at Chengdu Airport in front of a rather impressive Il-18. **Left** A view of the port outer 4250-ehp Ivchenko AI-20 turboprop belonging to Il-18 B-214 as the aircraft passes over Canton on long finals to Bai Yun (White Cow) Airport after a 1100 km, 1 hr 55 min flight from Chongking. On arrival a Human League pop cassette was being played over the PA system in an unprecedented outburst of bourgeoise liberalism

Overleaf Many Il-14 services are now being operated by An-24s and Xian-built Yun-7s. CAAC's original fleet of An-24s are slowly being upgraded to Yun-7 standard. B-3424 is parked in front of the control tower at Wu Su Airport, TaiYuan. **Inset** Even with all four engines removed B-206 still manages to look classy

Operated by the CAAC Industrial Aviation Corporation, based at Wu Su Airport, this Li-2 is still used for aerial survey work with at least three more Li-2s and eight Il-14s despite the advent of more modern equipment such as the Super King Air, Twin Otter and BO.105 helicopter

Right Despite the under-inflated tyres and the oil patches under the engines, and the fact that the aircraft appeared not to have been flown for some time, Li-2 No 303 seemed to be airworthy. The old Lanzhou Airport in the Yellow River valley (upper photo) is surrounded by mountains and CAAC decided to switch their operations to Zhongchuan Airport on the plateau above Lanzhou city

Above Dumped alongside a Tu-2 *Bat* bomber in the Aeronautical Compound of Peking University is this original DC-3 airframe, registration No 102, wearing very faded CAAC markings. The Compound also features an array of MiG fighters and trainers, a P-61 Black Widow and many other interesting exhibits

Below left Resplendent in full CAAC livery, this derelict Convair 240 can be found on the southern rim of Peking's Capitol Airport. The 240 entered service with American on 9 July 1946, paving the way for a succession of Convairliners (see Convair twins chapter, pages 68–81)

Right The Li-2 was a result of the Soviet Union obtaining a manufacturing license for the DC-3. Under the overall supervision of Boris Lisunov, such luminaries as Vladimir Myasishchev, I P Tolstykh and I P Mosolov set about making 1293 engineering changes to adapt the design for Soviet production. The most obvious change was the use of Shvetsov M-621R or M-63R 9-cylinder radials, often fitted with shutter-type cold-weather cowlings. This is another view of No 303 at Lanzhou, where at least ten Yun-5/An-2s (background) are in use for pilot training and utility tasks

Turboprops

Completed in March 1958, Manx Viscount
'Yankee Mike' looks as youthful as ever. Her
resale value will probably climb to around the £1
million-mark as she competes against the new
generation of commuterliners

Above Locked up for the afternoon at Luton, G-ARIR was originally built for Air France in June 1954 but came back on the British Register for Starways of Liverpool in 1961 to replace their DC-4. Returning to France with Air Inter, she later came back home to fly for Alidair out of their East Midlands and Aberdeen bases during the oil boom of the mid-seventies, and was seen painted in the colours of Inter City Airlines, an Alidair subsidiary, in June 1982. The 700-series Viscounts were usually recognized by the split rear cockpit window and the under-fuselage vent

Left The second Viscount 802 off the production line, 'Julie Bravo' takes a break at Heathrow in the autumn of 1973 wearing the then new temporary titles of British Airways over her previous BEA scheme. She worked for Scottish Division on the Highlands and Islands routes until superseded by the HS.748 in the early eighties

Much-modified Viscount 838 of the Royal Aircraft Establishment climbing out of Bournemouth after the annual air day in 1984. Based at Bedford, it is instantly recognizable by the 'raspberry ripple' scheme applied to most RAE aircraft. It was acquired by the MOD (PE) in 1965 having flown for Ghana Airways since new in 1961

Below Rotate! *Viscount Stephen Piercey* leaves Runway 35 at Aberdeen in September 1985 with a full load of oilmen bound for Shetland

Slim engine nacelles identify this Janus Viscount as a 700 series. Built for Trans Canada Airlines in a batch of fifteen 724s in 1954, she later flew with Air Inter and Alidair before becoming fire school fodder at Manston in Kent. Although wearing Janus titles at Exeter in early 1984, the small badge on the nose gives away the fact that she was occasionally flying for Guernsey Airlines

Right Guernsey Airlines' immaculate Vickers Viscount 806 operating out of Southend Airport on 12 November 1986. Currently registered G-BLOA, the aircraft was originally operated by BEA as G-AOYJ and registered as such in January 1958; it was later leased to Cyprus Airways in 1965. (Courtesy Gordon Bain)

Inside, outside: Viscount 814 G-BAPG receives
attention inside the West Country Aircraft
Servicing hangar on the north side of Exeter
Airport during April 1986, and (right) tailless,
engineless, and with a wheel missing, outside in
the Devon sunshine in November 1986

Left A laden Air Bridge 'Guardsvan' manoeuvres onto the ramp at Luton International in April 1985. On conversion to the freighter role, the Vanguard was officially named the Merchantman, but reversing its original name always seemed more appropriate. Powered by four Rolls-Royce Tyne turboprops, it arrived on the market just as the big jets made their entrance, and failed to be the success it deserved. Air Bridge are resurrecting more of these beautiful aeroplanes, the latest from EAS in Perpingnan

Above Merpati Nusantara Airlines of Indonesia bought this Vanguard from BEA, and it was photographed at the Heathrow Maintenance Base just before its delivery flight in 1974

Canadair built a derivative of the Britannia in the form of the CL-44 and powered it with Tyne eingines, too. It was the world's first swing-tail aircraft, and this Aer Turas Model CL-44D-4J EI-BGO was originally delivered to Loftleidir Icelandic Airlines in 1960. Specializing in bloodstock transport, Aer Turas operated a schedule for racehorse owners from Dublin to Luton, where this photograph was taken one quiet Saturday afternoon in October, 1980

Left EI-BGO nosing up to the camera on the cargo ramp at Dublin four years later, where it is now withdrawn from use, having been replaced by a lower time model in EI-BRP

A last look at Aer Turas' EI-BGO as she climbs
away from Bristol Airport, bound for Dublin with
some race horses after the Cheltenham Gold Cup
in March 1985

Jean machine: Wrangler's CL-44D-6 races off St
Croix's runway into the evening light enroute to
the mainland US. Collecting denims made in the
neighbouring island of St Thomas, it tech-stopped
regularly to take on cheaper gas at STX

Heavylift Cargo Airlines' unique CL-44, a
Conroy Guppy conversion of a standard CL-44D-
4, on short finals to land at Bristol Airport with a
cargo of race horses for the Cheltenham Gold Cup

Tail swung open, Heavylift's CL-44 Guppy
prepares to unload its precious cargo. **Overleaf**
Close-up of the monster hinges fitted to EI-BND

Steady boy! Thanks to its handler, this horse was persuaded to refrain from trampling the photographer

Right Aero Spacelines' Super Guppy 201, F-BPPA, is operated by Aeromaritime and spends most of its time ferrying Airbus parts from Britain and West Germany to the final assembly building in Toulouse. Based on the C-97J version of the Boeing Stratocruiser, the Super Guppy 201 is powered by 4912 ehp Allison 501-D22Cs and first flew on 24 August 1970. Vital statistics include a height of 48 ft 6 in, length of 143 ft 10 in, and a maximum takeoff weight of 170,000 lb; economical cruising speed is a stately 250 mph at 20,000 ft

Left A Balkan Bulgarian Il-18D passes the no waiting zone at Bristol Airport on its way back home in August 1982. Previously with Aeroflot, this aircraft is still in service with Balkan alongside six other sister ships some 21 years after it was built

Below Colourful L-188 Electra of Southeast Airlines pauses at Miami International in February 1978

Overleaf A Brit with a history. Taxying in at Exeter, strongly illuminated against a storm, 'Charlie Fox' was on a livestock charter to Italy in the winter of 1978. It was originally ordered by Northeast Airlines from the Bristol Aeroplane Co in 1958, but never delivered. It then went to Transcontinental of Argentina until its return to Britain in 1964 with British Eagle, during whose ownership it was converted to freight configuration. Monarch acquired it on Eagles' collapse and, after another spell abroad leased to African Cargo Airways, it was transferred to Invicta of Manston in whose service it is seen here. **Inset** Only part of the Britannia's 'stone age' flight deck—the engineer's panel is even worse. An electrician's nightmare, I am told, if anything goes tech. Note the rams horn control yoke, which has continued on Bristol aeroplanes into the supersonic age with Concorde

The RAF's 20-strong Britannia fleet came onto
the civil market in the wake of defence cuts in
1974. This one was flying for Gemini Air
Transport out of Luton in October 1980.
Below EI-BCI, owned by Aer Turas, worked for
Eurafric of Portugal

Convair twins

Supporters gather by the Norsk Metropolitan Klubb's Convair 440 at Eindhoven before their flight to Amsterdam after the great DC-3 50th anniversary meet in July 1985. An ex-SAS machine, this must be one of the most ambitious preservation projects yet to keep an airliner flying.

LN-KLK has standard Pratt & Whitney R-2800s, and can be seen visiting European airshows throughout the season. **Below** 'KLK unsticks at West Malling in Kent after a warbirds show, capturing the atmosphere of an overcast English day, which is slowly turning to rain

A view through the terrace garden at Beauvais during Paris *Salon* week. Visiting aircraft are not allowed to land at the show, and Beauvais, some 80 miles north of Paris, is a favourite alternative. Nor-Fly's Convair 440 waits for its passengers

Top right A more purposeful operation of the Convair 440 in recent years has been the regular shuttle operated between St Thomas and St Croix in the US Virgin Islands by American Airlines' subsidiary, American Inter Island. After the disastrous crash of an American Boeing 727 in a landing accident at St Thomas in the mid-seventies, the carrier refused to fly jets into St Croix until the airfield at St Thomas was improved. Hence, N827AA was one of five 440s operating the route, seen here taxying out at St Croix

Right Southern Express of Miami operate this Convair 440 with a fleet of Navajos and Bandeirantes

Overleaf A brush fire rages through the airfield boundary behind this American Inter Island Metropolitan at St Croix in April 1980. Light aircraft were rescued, but horses at the nearby racecourse stampeded when the flames overwhelmed their stables

Left Pictured in March 1985, this Convair 440 was built for Swissair as HB-IMN and first flew on 13 March 1957, named *Zug*. It was acquired by Pan Adria of Yugoslavia in 1969 and then sold in 1976 after a period of storage to Associated Products of America. One of the Convair's original competitors, a Martin 4-0-4, can be seen in the background among a lineup of business aircraft

Above Prinair purchased four Convair 580s to supplement their fleet of de Havilland Herons in 1981–82 before they replaced the Herons with the CASA C.212 Aviocar. N589PL, in a hybrid scheme, lifts off from St Thomas with the College of the Virgin Islands in the background

Overleaf Another quick turnround for N589PL as it disembarks passengers from San Juan, Puerto Rico, at St Thomas. Powered by 3750-ehp Allison 501 turbines, the 580's massive propellers are not unlike the sails of a Spanish windmill

XA-LOU began life in September 1953 as the KLM Convairliner 340 *Nicholaas Maes*, being transferred to ALM Dutch Antillean Airlines ten years later. Following a brief spell on the US register, she was sold to Aviateca in 1970, after which she was operated by Aerotur from Cancun in Mexico. When this photograph was taken in March 1985 the aircraft was in open storage at Opa Locka in Florida

Right Spit and polish! This immaculate US Navy VC-131F was one of a batch of 36 R4Y-1s manufactured between June 1955 and May 1956, and was approaching its 30th birthday when this picture was taken at Barbados in March 1985

An experimentally registered Convair 580 of the National Research Council of Canada at Juliana Airport on St Maarten in the Leeward Islands in December 1981. Originally a Model 440, the turbine conversion was carried out for owner Bethlehem Steel in 1965

Left Confirmed Convair of The Way International, a biblical research and teaching foundation from New Knoxville, Ohio, visited Bristol during its mission to the UK in the late seventies. A 580 converted from a Model 340, it started life with United Airlines in October 1952

Heavy recips

Decidedly static Douglas DC-4 N74183 at Fort Lauderdale minus No 3 engine. Built in 1944 for the USAAF, it flew on the Hungarian Airlift with Flying Tiger in 1956 and had accumulated 58,615 hr when it was retired by Pacific Western Airlines in 1972

Air Atlantique's DC-6 received its UK Certificate of Airworthiness on 7 April 1987 and began revenue-earning flights shortly afterwards. The aircraft was bought from Trans Continental Airlines and the 'Big Six' arrived at Coventry on 22 March 1987 after a 14 hr 20 min ferry flight from Gander, Newfoundland, having pre-positioned there from Willow Run Airport in Detroit, Michigan, the previous day

Below Seagreen Air Transport of Antigua leased this ex-Navy Douglas VC-118B from Paterson Aircraft to supplement their two DC-3s, a DC-6, a DC-7 and a Convair 880

Left The Jaguar in the foreground comes a poor second to the towering DC-6 of Air Atlantique. Freight doors open, a pristine 'X-ray Charlie' has an aura of understated efficiency. Built as a 'Pax' configuration DC-6B model, she made her maiden flight on 22 September 1958 and was delivered to Civil Air Transport, China, six days later, and went on to serve with CAAC before being transferred to Royal Air Lao in August 1968. After five years of operations with Air America and Air Asia, the aircraft was converted to 'A' status in Taiwan, where it was fitted with a strengthened floor and freight doors; the cabin windows were also blanked-off. Sold to Southern Air Transport of Miami in September 1973, she was subsequently acquired by Rosenberg Aviation Inc in June 1976 before joining Trans Continental in April 1978. At the time of writing (June 1987) G-SIXC had flown approximately 35,800 hr

This page Everything's looking good, so let's start No 1. OK, crack the throttle, squeeze the starter switches, wait for one-two-three-four-five-six blades, switch ignition to 'both' and depress the primer switch—there, she's caught. That big round R-2800 really is a wonderful engine. Stabilize at 800 rpm using primer fuel, then carefully increase the mixture as you're backing off on the primer. Nothing to it! (DC-6 N43872, Saarbrücken, May 1982)

A regal DC-7C, N74303 was delivered to Pan Am in July 1956 as *Clipper Ocean Rover*. Acquired by Club International in 1972, the aircraft still looked pretty smart in the maintenance area at Miami International some seven years later

A supposedly anonymous DC-6 rolls into San Juan Isla Verde on a wet morning in December 1981, but the registration (N928L) identifies it as one of the Bellomy Lawson fleet out of Miami

Flaps fully down, emergency windows open,
N841TA of Trans-Air-Link undergoes an outdoor
check in a corner of Miami International in
March 1985

Just relieved of its cargo of fruit and vegetables from the Dominican Republic, Dominicana DC-6B HI-92 takes time out before reloading for the return trip. The teeming masses of Puerto Rico are the market for the growers of Santo Domingo

Overleaf Heavy maintenance continues apace as a gaggle of DC-6s soak up the noon day sun at Miami. If R-2800s could burn kerosene instead of avgas, they'd probably go on forever

An Egret browses lazily in the scorched grass,
probably wondering why man makes this 'flight'
thing so complicated. DC-6 maintenance, Fort
Lauderdale, March 1985

The very low morning light catches this Connie half-asleep on the ramp at San Juan. TRADO used 749A Constellation HI-332 to haul fruit and vegetables for a short while in 1980

Top right HI-332 again: I think they've got the window cleaners in

Right Aerotours operated two 1049C Super Connies through San Juan, Dominican Republic, in 1979–80, HI-329 being one of them. They were a rare sight indeed, even in the late seventies, and once seen they were never forgotten. This Connie was built for Eastern Airlines and delivered in February 1954. It was converted to a freighter shortly after leaving Eastern, and even became a sprayer in 1974 before reverting to passenger operations

Overleaf Aerochago SA operated Super Constellation HI-228 into San Juan in January 1982, where the aircraft's cargo was unloaded one box at a time. Southern Flyer's DC-3s lurk in the background, and a Casair C-46 waits on the stand

One of the oldest Constellations in existence, N90816 sits at Fort Lauderdale like a hare in a field with its back to the wind. She was built for TWA as *Star of Geneva* in 1946 as an 049 series and, having survived the threat of destruction in a movie sequence in 1979, remains remarkably intact

Happy anniversary DC-3

That C-47's a C-53. Built as the troop carrying version of the faithful old Dak, it had no provision for heavy cargo and only a small passenger door. Flown by Aero Virgin Islands of St Thomas on routes between the islands and San Juan, it was eventually withdrawn from service in the early eighties

Happy Birthday! 50 years young and still going strong. Complete with commemorative markings, Air Atlantique's Dakota 4 G-AMSV flanks the Swedish Veteran's DC-3 SE-CFP (left) and warms up its two 1200 hp Pratt & Whitney R-1830 Twin Wasps prior to the six-ship flypast at Eindoven

Just like old times as Air Atlantique's DC-3
appears out of the mist on left base above the
lineup. Front to back we have the *Flygande
Veteraner* DC-3 SE-CFP, Confederate Air Force
R4D N151ZE, Air Luton G-AMPO, Dutch
Dakota Association PH-DDA and Hibernian
Dakota Flight N4565L

Left Reputedly the only surviving Navy R4D-6, N151ZE *Ready 4 Duty* flies the Confederate and Union flags from the cockpit roof escape hatch. Bet the skipper's arms get tired

What a beautiful paint job. Virgin Islands International Airways' DC-3-201D combines the hibiscus flower with the natural colours of the islands. N102AP was built for Eastern Airlines in September 1940 and the old girl is still as eager as ever

N102AP's sistership parked at St Thomas in complimentary colours. This standard C-47A has missed out on the panoramic passenger window mod

Top right Air Pennsylvania's DC-3 N2VM in a birova state at St Thomas, relegated to providing spares

Right Four Star Air Cargo C-47B takes a breather a STT in the shadow of the mountain which has brought so much disaster to the island, either by aircraft hitting it or by influencing the winds which produce so much shear on finals. In 1985, three C-47s operated alongside two Beech 18s and a DC-6A leased from Trans-Air-Link

More benign mountains provide the backdrop for a pair of Air BVI DC-3s on Beef Island Airport in 1980. VP-LVH, foreground, is the grand old lady of what must have been the world's most immaculate DC-3 fleet. 'Hotel was built at Santa Monica in July 1937 for American Airlines as *Flagship Philadelphia*, and co-author Austin Brown was at the wheel when she clocked up 65,000 flight hours on 14 June 1979. **Right** The front office of VP-LVH, but can a photograph communicate the feel of this wonderful machine?

Left Like a tired dog resting its head on someone's knee, Top Flight's Dakota G-ANAF peers over the top of G-AMHJ's rear fuselage. They, too, were both in the pound at Exeter in November 1986 when the company went into receivership

Overleaf Dakota G-AMPZ is owned by Exeter-based Harvest Air and works in an anti-pollution role under a government contract

Left Ex-G-AKNB, EI-BDU left the UK for the Emerald Isle in 1978 to fly with Dublin-based Clyden Airways. The Dakota undergoes engine checks on one of the wartime dispersals on the north side of Exeter Airport before delivery

This otherwise immaculate DC-3 of Bo-S-Air bears the familiar scars of a landing gear collapse at Charottle, North Carolina, in March 1985

Overleaf A snug fit in the parking lot at Miami International's cargo village in February 1977, this DC-3 had hopes of resurrection. Its wings were folded alongside

Above Somewhat squatter than usual, this poor DC-3 ran through the hedge at the upwind end of St Vincent's cul-de-sac runway at Arnos Vale Airport in early 1985

Left Luridly painted with images of Mexico, this wild Gooney was used for charters by a travel club out of Fort Lauderdale in the late seventies

Overleaf Air Cargo America's C-47B N10801 pauses a moment beside Caribou N544Y at San Juan International in November 1979. Beautifully polished, both aircraft delivered light cargo down-island into airfields that were too small for the big jets. The C-47 had previously served with the West German *Luftwaffe* for many years as CA+014

World of water

Avalon Aviation's Canso C-FHNH bears its planing bottom at Exeter in November 1986 between tanking contracts in Norway. Built in 1940 as a PBY-5A, this classic amphibian is powered by two Pratt & Whitney R-1820s, a powerplant which is also used by the C-47s parked in the background. The flowing lines of the hull add grace to a superbly executed design

The late Charles Blair brought his Sandringham flying boat back to the Solent in the summer of 1977. *Southern Cross* was moored off the old seaplane terminal at Calshot in waters reminiscent of its home base in the US Virgin Islands (in colour, if not in temperature)

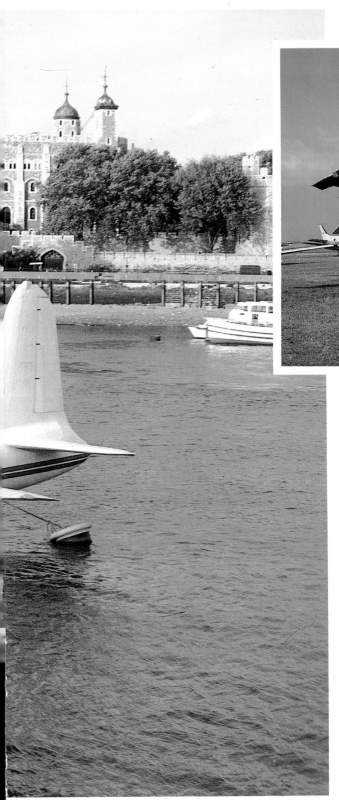

Edward Hulton achieved his ambition to bring his Sunderland through Tower Bridge into the Pool of London in October 1982, and he moored his majestic flying boat on the Thames with Traitor's Gate and the Tower of London in the background. This Sunderland worked alongside the Sandringham pictured on the preceding page for Antilles Air Boats and Ansett Airlines, cared for by the long-serving George Alcock (nephew of the great Sir John Alcock of transatlantic fame) and other fine engineers

Above From Goliath to David. This cute little Grumman Widgeon was sitting on the flight line at Tamiami Airport in March 1985. A five seater, it is the smallest of Grumman's family of twin-engined amphibians

Pitting its strength against the sea, a Grumman Mallard struggles to get on the step in Charlotte Amalie harbour en route to Christensted, St Croix, a service now provided by Virgin Islands Seaplane Shuttle. Once airborne it will have to avoid the yachts in its path until it climbs above mast-height